Between My Spine & The River

poems

Taylor Hamann Los

ISBN: 979-8-9914184-3-0

Ridge Books
www.eastridgereview.com

RIDGE
B O O K S

Table of Contents

What I Ask My Body For / 5

Migration / 6

Fairy Tale for Backwaters & Hesitant Mothers / 7

Etterath / 8

When You Say You Want to Try Again / 9

Self-Portrait as Storm Drain / 10

Anatomy of a Moth / 11

Root / 12

Ultrasound, 8 Weeks / 13

Linea Nigra / 14

My Husband Never Asks / 15

Dendrochronology / 16

Ghosts in Late August / 17

Third Trimester / 18

Watershed Lullaby / 20

Hysterectomy / 21

My Mother Says It Was Worth It / 22

Fever Dream / 23

If I Die / 24

Aubade for Tokophobia / 25

Notes / 26

Acknowledgments / 27

About the Author / 29

For Allison

What I Ask My Body For

For lemon trees grafted at my throat. For hydrangeas
in my blood to hum.

For stems to keep my organs tucked in their corners
like poems.

For surrender.

To open like oiled hinges, to be an orchard.

For satiety.

To swallow even my own bones—
once everything else is gone.

Migration

Movement of heron and cell—
        strange how a word can carry both.

Even stranger how a woman's body
        learns to carry: soft pull against her insides

that pulls until it ends in violence
        the way a fairy tale ends in something broken.

Were the women of the old stories
        ever this afraid? When I say *cervix*,

do I mean *neck* or *uterus*?
        One day, I'll say one and mean

the other. I know
        what my body's supposed to be for.

If fear is sharp, then I have
        given my neck to the guillotine.

That strange lure of flight—
        to surge across a gunmetal sky.

If this is a story, then in it,
        some women grow wings.

Fairy Tale for Backwaters & Hesitant Mothers

A woman walked into the forest
and never came out. In this wood,
there are eyes rimmed with pine
and brush and hunger so deep
it could bend bones. They say
she wanted a child, but her body
curled away from blood
and so she was swallowed
whole, her organs evanescing
one by one like mist on the creek's
stagnant waters. They say the trees
breathed her in, siphoning her life
because their own children perished
in the fire. Flames had cast their skeletal
remains to the forest floor—
this graveyard for squirrels and saplings.
And all that is left of the woman
is the timbre of leaves scratching against
their boughs. They say you can hear
rustling in the stillest of winters.
See, even the bark is weeping.

Etterath

I built a birdhouse on my chest,
nails driven into my breastbone,
skin puckering and gray at the edges.
A work of shoddy craftsmanship,
but, oh, I wanted to hear a warbler
sing right against my heart.

I lined the splintered cedar
with dried iris and cattail wisp—
this cradle for a birdling
still damp and unformed.

But the house and I both
remained empty except for a knock
and the echo of my own hand,
except where wood mites scrawled
their field notes along the walls.

When You Say You Want to Try Again

I understand this:
Islands are lost every day,
though the bony, bleached
parts of me will form
a new archipelago in water.

Most nights I pull only
nightmares from the harbor.
Gull and gut and salt,
a drowned Icarus.
I must wait for the storm
to leave my body
before I can put out
to sea, holes burned
in belly and sails.

I hunger for more
than smoked fish;
I have built you
from this ache.

Self-Portrait as Storm Drain

Even after collecting my grief and offering it to the river,
even after scraping through rust-coated prayers, I clatter like
metal against itself. My doctor hands me words like *common*
and *treatable*, but still I become a body distilled into what it
can and can't do, what hurts and what doesn't. This grate
inside I've failed to unlatch. I want to unlatch myself for you,
pull you into me like the rain, but I clog with oak leaves
raked in from the street. I am begging for mercy small as a
brook, staggering as an estuary—a dam against the ocean
muscling its salt into my throat.

Anatomy of a Moth

Your hand on my thigh
        after a glass of white wine

and I wish that I, too, could live
        without lungs. We seek spaces

in our bodies soft and dark;
        we emerge with crooked wings.

For you I will be translucent.
        Hold me up to the light.

Root

I

n. the usually underground part of a seed plant body

Wait in quiet darkness. Let parts of you push toward sun. Keep steady. Keep stretching further below.

II

n. the part of an organ or physical structure by which it is attached to the body

Become a garden. Thresh tissue from the field. Form fascia into stem.

III

n. something that is an origin or source

Understand that women are not just the soil but also the river. You will both plant and water.

IV

v. to fix or implant by or as if by roots

Plunge your feet into earth. Say, "This is the home I've made." Nurture the bulb inside your center.

V

v. to remove altogether by or as if by pulling out by the roots

You will know when it's ready. Let the seed detach with the wind. Let the seed become its own flower.

Ultrasound, 8 Weeks

Silent doppler,

>   flutters of my own birdseed heart,
>   kernels stuck to cardboard,

>   doctor
>   saying she was due
>   for a tricky one,

dimmed lights,

>   and, finally, chickadee on a screen,

>   breathing.

But reckless creatures
breed reckless things,

>   and I'm not sure what that means
>   for my child

except thirty-two more weeks

>   and spooning honey

>   between sunflower seeds

to keep each one
        from falling to the ground.

Linea Nigra

Mini meridian spanning my abdomen,
        dividing hemispheres, oceans, lakes.

My two lives, one before and one after.
        Vertical horizon line shivering with the

mulberry and cobalt hues of twilight.
        Rising edge of the palest moon.

I press my fingertips to my skin,
        the ripple of a tiny fist echoing back.

My Husband Never Asks

about the milkweed
in the refrigerator.
I don't tell him I want
to be a monarch,
that I bruise my knees
in prayer as the sun sheds
its chrysalis each evening.

I drip honey
on my wounds, bandage
them with box elder leaves.
These are my offerings.
Forgive me;
I have forgotten
how to speak, my tongue
thick with nectar.

Dendrochronology

After the anatomy scan, I dream
I can trace my daughter's growth
with my fingertips: rings
of muscle and amniotic fluid
and her body curled at my center.

One umbilical artery
where there should be two.
Too much *it's not a problem until it is.*

I dream I can write
her a different origin song,
one without drought,
without uncertainty. One with
the fullness of everything green,
more notes than we were promised.

Instead, I'll sing each stunted verse.
Cup my ear to listen for the tendrils
of her reply. I dream of soil
and water, of moth-ravaged leaves,
and there—suddenly—
the beginnings of a refrain.

Ghosts in Late August

Another night with owls and wooden gates swinging
toward every breeze and this fairy child testing the weight
of her wings in my womb. I haven't slept in weeks.

We make love with the lights on: you against me
against sheets we keep saying we'll replace and never do.
I open the windows and crickets tumble inside.

I remember the story of a girl who tied a lily stem
to her ribs as she lay dying on the forest floor.
When they went to dig her up the next spring,

they found a meadow of blood-stained flowers.
I ask if you remember this story too, but you only
brush away the wings littering the dresser.

Tomorrow will bring more of the same. Maybe we'll find
that field of flowers and then head home just to leave
the lights on again. We won't change the sheets.

We'll wonder how many times a sparrow can beat
against the window before her heart fails, why
the promise of light brings her over and over again.

Third Trimester

Today is the anniversary of your heart
        stopping,

and I am every poem I've never read.
        Elemental,

a body bursting with colors and sounds
        and light.

When I drove you home from the hospital,
        we

joked about how you beat me to the first
        ultrasound,

how the gray image with underwater gurgle
        made you

a lake. Now I've become one too,
        cradling

in my waters more than just fish
        and shells.

Funny how a life can be stripped down,
        measured

by shaky lines on paper, circles moving away
        from center.

I could write a book from these
ripples.

Watershed Lullaby

—For my daughter

Hush—let the waters flush out the valley
and slip through grass as silently as down
a window pane. Let dreams rush from where they
stay tucked until the day filters its light.
Sleep—let stars constellate behind your eyes.
Let warm earth cradle you until the time
when pre- transmutes to post-, when you and I
are primal enough to finally meet.
I will look for you in the curve between
my spine and the river, between cascade
and every small heartbeat. Soon, I will
carry you home, ask the rain for your name.
But what do we know of the rain? Only
that home is the muscle aching with rain.

Hysterectomy

Cut out the womb. Replace it with a beehive,
small fist nestled in the hollow of the body.

Or leave it empty as marriage vows
broken against the thighs of another woman.

Forgive this mess—*sterile* doesn't always mean
clean the way a husband doesn't always come home.

All the soft parts of the body begging to be touched
crumble—a thousand tiny landslides.

Look at this menagerie of bones:
honeycomb cathedral begging for light.

My Mother Says It Was Worth It

Those nineteen hours, the blood—all of it—
but I never wanted to be a violent daughter.
To her, it didn't matter that the doctor had to sew
her body back together with a needle and thread
or that the stain took months to fade.

I blame Eve for everything—the way I lie
here torn like fruit flesh in the orchard, ants
swarming. The way I tremble at every gloved hand.

Eve asked for a place to hide her darkness.
Her body split and offered it to her: two sons,
one stone. But I gape with the hollowness of empty night,
no longer a body-temple but a basin for fallen rain.

Fever Dream

Sheets stick with sweat, and I swear
I can see God as my body burns.

Or maybe it's just this strange creature
I've dreamt again, wings beating

a reminder that I haven't felt holy in years.
I arch toward the ceiling fan,

pray for a stone to scrape salt
from skin or for the flush of cool tiles.

Through a sliver of window, light
kaleidoscopes the wall.

Here on the bed, a revelation.
In the bathroom, a sink full of angels.

If I Die

before my daughter
wakes, then strew her cradle
with lilies so she knows
they mean more than a burial.
Leave a ladleful of soup
cooling in the bowl. She'll ask
who it's for, so tell her
that her mother never believed
in ghosts but wondered
about them sometimes.
Teach her to listen with ear
to earth for the lullabies
underneath. Tell her
to always pick up the cats
with both hands. Leave a jar
in the yard for fireflies.
And when she's grown,
tell her that if I could,
I would pull my bones
up, rising to the surface
just to meet her.

Aubade for Tokophobia

Let me depart without sorrow, with the stale crust of winter sticking in my ribs. Let me knit myself back together as a woman who has never held a needle, never pushed it through her own skin in search of relief. The dawn is messy and I am messy and I think for once that might not matter. There will always be walleye and oil in the pan, a placenta rupturing, a child asking who you were before her. There will always be some kind of lover left out with the trash, an egg dripping down the sides of the can. And one day, the child will ask again. I will tell her I was a velvet curtain at dusk, my edges not quite covering the window.

Notes

All definitions in "Root" are from *Merriam-Webster.*

"If I Die" is inspired by the tomb of Maria Magdalena Langhans, sculpted by Johann August Nahl in 1751.

Acknowledgments

First and foremost, Thank you to the editors of the journals in which these poems first appeared, sometimes in different versions:

Anti-Heroin Chic: "Etterath." *CLOVES Literary*: "Aubade for Tokophobia," "Self-Portrait as Storm Drain." *Crow & Cross Keys*: "Fairy Tale for Backwaters & Hesitant Mothers." *East Ridge Review*: "My Husband Never Asks," "What I Ask My Body For," "When You Say You Want to Try Again" (republication). *Eunoia Review*: "Linea Nigra"; "Root"; "Ultrasound, 8 Weeks"; "Watershed Lullaby." *Moist Poetry Journal*: "Anatomy of a Moth." *Parentheses Journal*: "Migration." *Rust + Moth*: "When You Say You Want to Try Again." *Stone Circle Review*: "Dendrochronology." *The Shore*: "Ghosts in Late August."

Thank you to God for giving me this life. I owe everything to you.

Lukasz, thank you for being both the love of my life and my best friend. Allison, my beautiful girl, thank you for giving my life a new purpose. Mom and Dad, thank you for your unconditional love and support. Mikayla and Elizabeth, thank you for being the best sisters I could ever ask for.

Thank you also to those I am happy to call my poetry friends, who helped me revise many of these poems:

Cynthia Bernard, Aubrey Brady, Karen Bramblett, and Daniel Schall. You guys are amazing.

Thank you to the incredible professors of Lindenwood University's MFA program for their guidance, support, and insightful feedback.

And finally, thank you to A.R. Williams for bringing this book into the world. It means everything to me.

About the Author

Taylor Hamann Los is a poet and copy editor from Wisconsin. Her poetry has appeared in *Magma Poetry*, *Tinderbox Poetry Journal*, *The Shore*, *Parentheses Journal*, *Split Rock Review*, and elsewhere. Her work has been nominated for Best of the Net, and she holds an MFA from Lindenwood University and an MLIS from UW-Milwaukee. You can find her on X/Twitter (@taylorhamannlos), Instagram (@taylorhlos_poetry), and at taylorhamannlos.wordpress.com.

www.ingramcontent.com/pod-product-compliance
Lightning Source LLC
Chambersburg PA
CBHW051742040426
42447CB00008B/1266